Contents

CW00429343

Introduction

Children have a natural desire to tell stories. If adults can help children to put their thoughts into words in story form, then children's ability to structure and come to terms with a wide world of real and imaginary experiences will be enhanced. This book aims to help adults in a variety of pre-school settings to develop children's innate interest in, and need for, telling stories – both their own and other people's.

Developing story-telling skills
Children naturally begin making up stories as they talk to themselves during their play. Gradually, if children have the opportunity to hear many stories being told, and to share books with adults, they begin to develop an awareness of 'audience' and of the pleasure involved in telling a story for others to hear. This can be in the form of an oral account, by 'reading' a book to a friend or a toy, through the use of puppets or in fantasy and role-play. Each time an adult asks a child to recall and describe what happened, for example, in the home-corner, the child becomes, in effect, a story-teller, especially if the adult writes down the child's words in narrative form.

Early Learning Goals
Story-telling skills are integral to the Language and Literacy component of the Early Learning Goals for children aged four plus in nursery

settings. The activities in this book involve the children in listening carefully to stories and are designed to help them to develop their own ability to make up stories which others may hear. Developing story-telling skills at this stage can also promote children's creative and personal and social skills. The abilities to empathize with story characters, act out roles, and work in a small group, sharing ideas and speaking in turn, will boost confidence and enhance feelings of self-esteem.

Baseline Assessment
Baseline Assessment schemes are designed to provide a link between the nursery curriculum and the programmes of study of the National Curriculum. Baseline Assessments of children in the area of language and literacy require judgements of children's competence in relation to performance descriptions of speaking and listening skills. The activities in this book are designed to help children to develop the skills of speaking in a group as they begin to extend their ideas and stories, by providing some detail such as descriptions of events, places, characters and feelings.

How to use this book
The book contains fourteen double-page spreads of activity ideas. The left-hand page of each spread provides a practical activity using

resources which are readily available in most early years settings. Each activity explains how the children can use the photocopiable sheet on the right-hand side of the spread, how to assess the children's understanding of the activity and how to involve parents in their child's learning. The photocopiable activity which consolidates the learning can also serve as an assessment record of each child's individual achievement. The ideas are aimed at four-year-olds with support and extension ideas for younger or more able children. There is a photocopiable Skills development chart on the final page of the book, forming a pictorial record of the sequence of skills developed in the book. Ask each child to colour in each activity on the chart as they complete them, then place the chart in the child's record of attainment folder.

Progression

There is a gradual progression of difficulty in the activities, starting with the concrete and leading towards the development of imaginative thinking. The activities are designed to develop children's ability to link events based on incidents, characters, location and feelings in oral form. An adult can then either scribe the child's ideas for them or assist the child in using emergent writing to record their ideas.

The activities develop the following story-telling skills:
• linking incidents based on events, characters, locations and feelings
• using traditional story beginnings
• making up alternative endings for well-known stories
• structuring a story
• thinking up names for story characters
• making up fantasy stories.

Home links

At the end of each activity there is a suggestion for a consolidation and/or extension activity for parents and carers to carry out with their child at home. These suggestions can form a useful part of Baseline Assessment procedures. They are designed to involve parents in their child's learning and are intended to develop a range of story-telling skills.

Occasionally, make a tape recording of a child telling a story and send it home with a suggestion that the child may like to record another story at home, to be brought back and played in your setting. Put up a notice inviting parents to record themselves making up a short bedtime story about their child which they and their child might enjoy sharing with the other children in the group.

Guess what happened!

Learning objective
To make up a story in response to two pictures.

Group size
Four children.

What you need
Scissors; thick card; transparent covering film; glue; pencils; a copy of the photocopiable sheet for each child and one A3 sized copy.

Preparation
Cut out the pictures from the enlarged photocopiable sheet, mount them on thick card, and cover with film.

What to do
Divide the cards into two sets – one containing the pictures of the boy, girl, dog and bird, and the other containing the balloon, apple tree, puddle and sandpit. Place the two sets face downwards on the floor. Sit the children in a circle around the piles. Let each child in turn take one card from each pile, place them face upwards, side by side, on the floor, and say, 'Guess what happened!'. The rest of the group should respond by saying 'What happened?'. The first child then makes up a simple story about the two pictures.

Individual recording
Give each child a copy of the photocopiable sheet. Ask them to cut out the two pictures that they used in the game, and to stick them in the two blank spaces on their sheet. Underneath the pictures, scribe each child's story for them to overwrite or copy. Use the back of the sheet if necessary.

Support
Scribe the children's stories for them.

Extension
Ask each child to write their story using their own level of emergent spelling.

Assessment
Check the child's ability to respond to the pictures by placing a different card from the second pile next to his card from the first pile. Ask him to make up a new story, seeing if he can adapt his original story by interpreting the second picture. Repeat, using a new first card next to the card from the second pile.

Home links
Encourage parents to help their child at home by cutting out two pictures from a pre-school comic, magazine or children's greetings card, sticking them onto paper, and encouraging their child to make up a story about them. Ask them to let their children bring the pictures in to retell the story to the group.

Guess what happened!

And then...

Learning objective
To verbalize a story with up to three incidents, using the link phrase 'and then...'.

Group size
Up to five children.

What you need
A toy dog; rubber bone; small rolled-up newspaper; bowl of dog biscuits; large card picture of a dog kennel; slipper; blanket; easel or board; scissors; Blu-Tack; glue; a copy of the photocopiable sheet for each child and one enlarged copy.

Preparation
Cut out the pictures from the enlarged photocopiable sheet. Arrange the toy dog and the props randomly on the blanket on the floor.

What to do
Sit the children around the blanket. Choose three of the props and the dog and place them by the easel, where the children can see them. Make up a story about the dog involving the props, holding up each one at the appropriate time, and using the phrase 'and then...'. Tell the story slowly once more, this time sticking the relevant picture on the easel, and encouraging the children to join in the phrases 'and then...'.

Now ask each child to choose three props and to make up a simple story, holding up each item at the appropriate time and using the phrase 'and then...'.

Individual recording
Encourage each child to cut out the three pictures from the photocopiable sheet which illustrate the story that they told and to stick them in the correct order on the sheet, verbalizing the story as they do so.

Support
Ask each child to point to the relevant picture on the sheet as you retell them their story. Help

them to cut out and stick down their pictures and to say what is happening in each one, miming the actions.

Extension
As the children stick down their pictures in order, encourage them to use the terms 'first', 'second' and 'third'. For example: 'the first thing that the dog did was to..., and then the second thing was to...'.

Assessment
Check that the child can retell incidents using the phrase 'and then...' by encouraging her to talk about, for example, the sequence of getting up, getting dressed, having breakfast and so on.

Home links
Give each child a strip of paper, folded into three sections to take home. Ask parents to help their children draw pictures, in order, of three events that happened over the weekend. Ask the children to bring the pictures back to your group to talk about them.

And then...

The lost teddy

Learning objective
To make up a story using props.

Group size
Four children.

What you need
A teddy bear; pretend bed or child's camp-bed; toy-box; two large cardboard boxes; ruler; black felt-tipped pen; scissors; sticky tape; glue; playbricks or small food cartons (emptied and cleaned); four tea trays; play people; crayons; a copy of the photocopiable sheet for each child.

Preparation
Turn the cardboard boxes into a wardrobe and a chest of drawers by drawing appropriate lines and knobs with a black felt-tipped pen. Set up an area to resemble a child's bedroom, with the bed, toy-box, wardrobe and chest of drawers. Hide the teddy bear somewhere in the area.

What to do
Sit the children facing the 'bedroom'. Choose one child to look for the lost teddy bear, and another child to describe the first child's actions to the rest of the group using such phrases as '...looked behind the wardrobe', '...looked

under the bed' and so on. When the bear has been found, hide it again and let the next pair of children have a go at finding it and describing the actions.

Individual task
Give each child a copy of the photocopiable sheet. Encourage them to colour in the bear and the furniture and to cut out the pictures. Ask each child to stick the pictures onto appropriately-sized playbricks or small food cartons using sticky tape and/or glue, to make 3-D manoeuvrable items. Encourage each child to arrange their items on a tea tray in front of them to make a 'bedroom', and then to 'hide' the bear. Give each child a play person and encourage the child to make up a story about the play person looking for the bear.

Support
'Hide' the bear on the child's tray 'bedroom' and ask them to move their person according to your instructions, for example 'look under the bed', 'look inside the wardrobe' and so on.

Extension
Ask the children to think of further places in the bedroom where the bear could be hidden, and to design these items. They could include a paper rug, a radiator made from corrugated paper for the bear to 'fall behind', a bin made from the lid of an aerosol can, a bookcase made from Sticklebricks and so on.

Assessment
Check that the child can make up 'lost item' stories involving scenarios with specific hiding places such as a kitchen, living room, garden, park or farm.

Home links
Ask parents to play a simple game of 'hide-and-seek' with their children at home, with the adults hiding and the children verbalizing where they are looking.

The lost teddy

A busy day

Learning objective
To tell a story using 'I', involving three locations.

Group size
Five children.

What you need
A large open area; a 'sit-and-ride' car; tables; card; felt-tipped pens; pencils; scissors; books; toy fruit; shopping bag; writing pad; telephone; four chairs; doctor's coat; a copy of the photocopiable sheet for each child.

Preparation
In a large open area, create a 'library', 'fruit shop', 'doctor's surgery' and 'home', using tables, labelled cards and a few props. Arrange the tables in the same way as drawn on the sheet. Place one chair behind each 'building'.

What to do
Explain that one child at a time is going to have a busy day driving around and visiting various buildings. They must then go home and tell a friend where they have been, in the correct order, and what happened at each place.

Ask one child to sit on each chair behind the library, shop and doctor's surgery. They will be the librarian, shopkeeper and doctor. Choose one child to sit in the 'sit-and-ride' car and make a journey, stopping off at the library, fruit shop and the doctor's surgery and having a short conversation with the librarian, shopkeeper and doctor. When the 'driver' has visited all three buildings, encourage them to drive 'home' and sit on the chair. Now choose another child to

visit the driver, who should recount the journey in the correct order.

Let each child have a go at being the 'driver', choosing their own order of visits.

Individual recording
Ask each child to recount their journey to you using their copy of the photocopiable sheet, making a pencil line of the journey around the buildings as they do so.

Support
Let the children use a small toy car to trace their journey along the sheet instead of a pencil.

Extension
Let older children think of three different locations each. Give each child three white peel-off labels and felt-tipped pens. Invite them to draw their new buildings and to stick the labels on top of the original buildings on their sheet to create a new journey to talk about.

Assessment
Can the child talk about the journey in the correct order? Does he use phrases such as 'then', 'after that' and 'next'?

Home links
Send home a strip of paper folded into five sections. Ask parents to encourage their child to draw three landmarks passed on the journey home from your group each day, with your setting in the first section and the child's house in the last section. Ask parents to help their child talk about the journey.

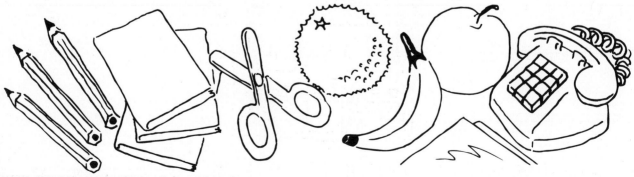

A busy day

Let's begin!

Learning objective
To practise beginning a story with 'Once upon a time...', 'One night...' and 'One morning...'.

Group size
Up to four children.

What you need
Three shopping bags or shoeboxes; a crown; toy frog; soft toy owl and baby owl (or pictures drawn on card); postperson's hat; parcel wrapped in brown paper, with stamps and address; selection of story-books with the above openings; pencils; a copy of the photocopiable sheet for each child.

Preparation
Put the crown and frog in one bag, the owls in another bag, and the postperson's hat and parcel in the remaining bag.

What to do
Talk about how stories often begin with 'Once upon a time...', 'One night...', 'One morning...' and so on. Look through some of the story-books and find examples of stories beginning with each opening. Explain that when a story begins with 'Once upon a time...' it is usually a fairy-tale, a magic story from a long time ago.

Sit the children in a circle and introduce the prop bags. In turn, ask each child to choose a bag and to remove the props. Encourage them to choose an appropriate opening depending on the bag that they have chosen, and to make up a simple story using the props.

Individual recording
Give each child a copy of the photocopiable sheet. Help each child to read the story openings and to draw a line to the picture of the appropriate story, continuing to tell the story to the adult. Scribe the story on the back of the sheet for each child.

Support
Cut out two small moon, sun and crown symbols from card. Before completing the photocopiable sheet, ask the child to place each symbol by the appropriate picture. Read the story openings to the child, then encourage them to place the matching symbol next to the appropriate openings.

Extension
Help the children to make up their own stories with appropriate openings, for example 'One rainy day...', 'One snowy morning...'.

Assessment
Ask the child how she would begin stories about an owl, a postperson and a prince/princess. Now ask for story openings about a bat, somebody having breakfast and a castle. Can the child think of more examples on her own? Does she understand that the way a story begins can tell us about when it happened, for example, 'a long time ago', 'at night', or 'in the morning'?

Home links
Ask parents to help their children find a story beginning with 'Once upon a time...' and to bring it in to your group. Make a display of the different stories.

Let's begin!

Once upon a time

One morning

One night

On the farm

Learning objective
To make up a story based on a rhyme or song.

Group size
Five children.

What you need
Pictures of farm animals; a toy farm with play people and animals; drawing materials; a copy of the photocopiable sheet for each child.

Preparation
Display the pictures of farm animals at child height. Arrange the toy farm animals into groups on the farm, being 'looked after' by the play people.

What to do
Discuss the pictures and talk about the noises that the different farm animals make. Let the children practise making the noises. Now talk about how people look after the different farm animals, for example feeding the ducks, milking the cows, collecting the eggs from the chickens, grooming the horses, shearing the sheep and so on. Sing 'Old MacDonald Had a Farm', encouraging the children to join in with the animal sounds. When they are confident with the song, sing an alternative version, using different children's names and referring to jobs that they might do on a farm:
Jahan Hussain went to a farm
E–I–E–I–O!
And on that farm he fed some ducks...
...And on that farm he milked some cows...
...And on that farm he sheared some sheep... .

Encourage the children to join in with the actions and sounds for each verse.

Individual recording
Ask each child to draw him or herself in each picture on their photocopiable sheet, carrying out a different farm activity. Encourage them to point to the pictures as they sing the alternative version of the song, using their own name.

Support
Talk about how to look after the different farm animals. Help the children to decide what to draw, then encourage them to 'talk through' their pictures with you.

Extension
Ask the children to sing the rhyme 'Jack and Jill' using their own name and that of a friend, and then to draw the story on a strip of paper divided into four sections.

Assessment
Can the child tell a simple story about himself visiting a farm, talking about what he did, and the noises that the animals made?

Home links
Ask parents to send in a head-and-shoulders photograph of their child. Photocopy and enlarge each one, cut it out, and stick it onto the upper part of a large piece of paper. Invite each child to draw in the rest of their body, and other details to show them looking after their chosen farm animal. Let the child dictate or write a caption. Use the children's pictures to make a display.

On the farm

In the end

Learning objective
To think of alternative endings for well-known fairy-tales.

Group size
Up to six children.

What you need
Traditional versions of 'The Gingerbread Man' and 'Little Red Riding Hood'; a small blackboard easel or whiteboard easel; coloured chalk or marker pens; Blu-Tack; drawing materials; a copy of the photocopiable sheet for each child and one copy enlarged to A3 size.

Preparation
Cut out the individual sections from the enlarged photocopiable sheet. Attach them to the easel with Blu-Tack in the correct order, leaving a blank section at the end.

What to do
Over two sessions, read the children the traditional versions of 'The Gingerbread Man' and 'Little Red Riding Hood'. When you have finished each story, ask how the children feel about what happened in the end. Do they feel happy or sad? Can they think of alternative endings? For example, the gingerbread man might escape, and the fox might apologize for trying to eat him!

Show the children the pictures on the easel. Talk about what is happening in each picture, then invite them to suggest alternative endings for the last section. As each child suggests an ending, draw it in the blank space for everyone to see. 'Read' the entire story, incorporating the new ending. Erase each picture prior to drawing the next suggestion.

Individual recording
Give each child a copy of the photocopiable sheet. Ask them to draw their own picture of their alternative ending in the blank section at the end of each story.

Support
Encourage the children to suggest the endings for their stories. Draw a section of the picture for each child and invite them to complete the details.

Extension
Encourage older children to add captions or speech bubbles to the characters in their picture.

Assessment
Note whether the child can effectively make up a new ending for a story. Talk about which endings she prefers for each story, and why. Talk about being 'fair'.

Home links
Ask parents to talk to their child about an alternative ending for another traditional story, such as 'Goldilocks and the Three Bears', and to jot down the ending for their child to bring to the group. Stick these in a large sugar-paper book entitled 'In the end', and invite the children to illustrate it.

In the end

Oh dear!

Learning objective
To tell a story about an accident, using the structure 'One day..., and then..., and in the end...'.

Group size
Up to four children.

What you need
A copy of the photocopiable sheet for each child plus one copy enlarged to A3 size; card; glue; scissors; crayons; clothes line; pegs; paper; drawing materials.

Preparation
Mount the enlarged copy of the photocopiable sheet onto card and cut out the pictures. Suspend the washing line.

What to do
Peg up the pictures in the correct order on the clothes line. Tell the story, using the link phrases 'One day...', 'and then...' and 'in the end...', pointing to each card at the appropriate time.

Retell the story, encouraging the children to join in with the link phrases. Choose one child at a time to peg up the cards in the correct order and tell the story, with the rest of the group joining in.

Individual recording
Using the pictures on the photocopiable sheet, ask each child to read the link phrases with you, but to describe what happens in each picture using their own words. Now ask each child to draw themselves in the story on a blank sheet and to retell the story, this time about themselves. Scribe their story for them.

Support
Encourage younger children simply to talk through the story on the photocopiable sheet.

Extension
Give older children a white sticky label to cover up the picture of the bicycle, and ask them to draw something else that a child might fall over. Ask them to add details to the first picture to show where the story took place, such as a garden, park or beach. Then ask each child to retell the story, reading the link phrases and describing the pictures.

Assessment
Assess whether the child can tell a story using the link phrases by making up a joint story. Provide a boy doll and a girl doll, a book and a stone. Ask the child to choose a doll and to think of a name, and then to choose either the book or the stone and to retell the story in which the doll falls over the book or stone. Provide support as the child tells the story, and check that he is using the link phrases.

Home links
Ask parents to cut a cartoon strip from a weekend newspaper, and to cover up the speech bubbles. Encourage them to help their child tell the story in his or her own words.

Oh dear!

One day

and then

and then

and in the end

Weather feelings

Learning objective
To tell a story involving feelings.

Group size
Four children.

What you need
Card; felt-tipped pens; scissors; glue; crayons; easel; Blu-Tack; paper; a copy of the photocopiable sheet for each child.

Preparation
Cut the card into three rectangles, each measuring 38cm x 28cm. On each rectangle, draw a picture of the sun, rain and a rainbow respectively. Make two A3 size copies of the photocopiable sheet, and colour the pictures the same on both sheets. Stick one enlarged copy onto the easel with Blu-Tack, and cut out the pictures from the other.

What to do
Hold up the pictures of the sun, rain and rainbow one at a time. Ask the children how each picture makes them feel, and why. Encourage the children to make an appropriate facial expression as you hold up each card. Give each child one of the cut out enlarged pictures from the story sequence. Ask them in turn to say what is happening in the picture, and how they think the boy and girl might be feeling. Now ask each child to stick their picture on top of the matching picture on the easel using Blu-Tack.

Individual recording
Encourage each child to cut out the pictures on their photocopiable sheet and arrange them in the correct sequence on the table as they tell you the story. Give each child a blank sheet of paper and ask them to stick the pictures down in the correct order. Let them colour in the finished sequence.

Support
Cut out the pictures for the children, and number them from 1 to 4. Help the children to lay out the pictures in the correct order by talking about what happens first in the story, second and so on, and asking the child to point to the number at the bottom of each picture. Write the numbers from 1 to 4 on a blank piece of paper and help the children stick the pictures in the correct places.

Extension
When the children have stuck down their pictures in the correct order, ask them to number each picture at the bottom and then to cut out the pictures. Encourage them to make a 'cover' with a title and staple the pages together to make a book.

Assessment
Can the child make up a story about the weather, talking about whether it makes her feel happy, sad, cross or surprised?

Home links
Send home two sets of hand-drawn peel-off stickers – one set of weather symbols (rain, sun, cloud and snow) and one set of facial expressions (happy, sad, excited, angry). Ask parents to make a small chart at home, over a period of time, relating the weather to their child's mood. Encourage them to write why their child felt sad or happy.

Weather feelings

Think of a name

Learning objective
To think of names for animal characters.

Group size
Four children.

What you need
A toy elephant, dog, bear and rabbit; role-play fire helmet, workman's hard hat, police helmet and chef's hat; aluminium foil; card; Blu-Tack; scissors; glue; crayons; lolly sticks; sticky tape; a copy of the photocopiable sheet for each child.

Preparation
Stick the children's photocopiable sheets to individual sheets of card. Cover the workman's hard hat in aluminium foil to make a space helmet. Place the toy animals at one side of a table and the hats at the other side.

What to do
Sit the children around the table. Talk about the different hats and who might wear them. Invite the children to experiment putting a different hat onto each animal and then to think of a name for each animal according to the job that they might do while they are wearing the hat.

For example, Police officer Rachel Rabbit, Firefighter Ellie Elephant, Astronaut Dennis Dog, Chef Ben Bear and so on.

Individual recording
Ask each child to colour the hats and animal heads on the photocopiable sheet and then cut along the lines to make individual pictures. Show the children how to stick their animal heads onto lolly sticks using sticky tape to make puppets. Let the children stick the hats onto the animals' heads using Blu-Tack to create the characters that they talked about together beforehand.

Support
Make the stick puppets and hats for the children and challenge them to find the correct hat as you describe an animal character and its job.

Extension
Let older children make more hats for their animals to represent different jobs. Ask them to make up new names for their animal puppets, and to tell simple stories about their jobs.

Assessment
How inventive is the child? Can he think of names beginning with the same sound, for example, Police officer Pete, Firefighter Fiona and so on?

Home links
Send home a simple hat, such as a crown, for the children to put on their favourite soft toy. Ask parents to help their child think of a special name for the toy in its new role. Encourage the children to bring in their toys to make up stories about and to use in puppet shows.

Think of a name

Bear feelings

Learning objective
To empathize with the feelings of a story character.

Group size
Up to four children.

What you need
Four paper plates; sugar paper; scissors; felt-tipped pens; sticky tape; kitchen roll tubes; a saucepan; wooden spoon; three chairs; a blanket; a copy of the photocopiable sheet for each child.

Preparation
Draw Mummy Bear's face onto each of the paper plates looking happy, sad, surprised and cross. Stick on triangular 'ears' made from sugar paper. Stick a tube to each plate to make masks that the children can hold.

What to do
Explain that when things happen in a story it can make the people in the story feel happy, sad, cross or surprised. Talk to the children about Mummy Bear's changing feelings as she makes the porridge, realizes that it's too hot, sees Baby Bear's broken chair and watches Goldilocks running away. Show the children the masks and talk about each of the expressions. Invite them to tell you when they have felt happy, sad, cross or surprised.

Now invite one child to pretend to be Mummy Bear and to act out the various incidents. Encourage them to hold up the appropriate Mummy Bear mask as you narrate the events.

Individual recording
Give each child a copy of the photocopiable sheet. Talk about how Mummy Bear would feel in each situation, and then encourage the children to draw the appropriate expression on her face in each picture. Ask the child to say why she feels as she does. For example, she might feel sad when Goldilocks runs away because she wanted to look after Goldilocks until her family came to fetch her.

Support
Draw the four expressions on circular peel-off stickers, for the children to stick on the sheet.

Extension
Make four card labels – 'happy', 'surprised', 'cross' and 'sad' – and ask each child to place a label in the appropriate square on the sheet.

Assessment
Can the child explain Mummy Bear's feelings in terms of what happens in the story? Can she relate these feelings to any experiences in her own life?

Home links
Send home small four-page blank books with beginning captions for parents and children to complete. For example, (child's name) is happy when...; (child's name) is sad when...; (child's name) is surprised when...; (child's name) is cross when... . The children can draw the pictures during their time at the group.

Bear feelings

In a cottage in a wood...

Learning objective
To imagine and to describe where story characters live.

Group size
Up to six children.

What you need
Copies of the traditional stories 'The Three Little Pigs', 'The Three Billy Goats Gruff', 'Sleeping Beauty' and 'Snow White'; bricks; construction sets; small empty food packets; sticky tape; play people; troll-type figure; three toy pigs; three toy goats; card; scissors; a copy of the photocopiable sheet for each child.

Preparation
Set out the bricks and construction sets, play people, troll-type figure and the three toy pigs and goats.

What to do
Over a few sessions, read the children the traditional stories. Talk about where the people and animal characters live, inviting the children to look at the pictures in the book for ideas. Talk about what each house might have been made from. Encourage the children to look at the bricks and construction sets. Help them to

decide what they might use to build a brick house for the three little pigs to live in together at the end of the story, a bridge where the troll used to live, Sleeping Beauty's palace, and the cottage for the seven dwarfs.

Encourage the children to have a go at making the different types of homes using the construction sets and bricks.

Individual recording
Let each child cut out the pictures of the homes on the photocopiable sheet and stick them onto the front or side of bricks or small empty food packets to make 3-D models. Let them use these with the play people and animals to talk through the stories.

Support
Make the model homes for the children and ask them to match the homes with the appropriate small-world items.

Extension
Let older children make small cardboard story characters. Show them how to stick a straw to the back of each character to make a rod puppet. Let the children create fields, forests and so on around their homes, using green sugar paper, kitchen rolls and junk materials.

Assessment
Check that the child is able to describe where a toy animal lives by using a selection of soft toys and asking him to tell you where each one might live. Encourage him to go into detail by using prepositions and adjectives, for example, 'near a wooden bridge', 'in the middle of a dark forest', 'at the end of a twisty path' and so on.

Home links
Send home a small story play figure or animal one night or over the weekend. Ask parents to help their child build a special home using their own construction toys. Include a strip of paper to be sent back saying, 'I made a... home for...'.

In a cottage in a wood...

It's magic!

Learning objective
To invent a magical story.

Group size
Up to six children.

What you need
A copy of the photocopiable sheet for each child and one copy enlarged to A3 size; card; glue; glitter; scissors; Blu-Tack; stapler; felt-tipped pens; pencils; board or easel.

Preparation
Stick the enlarged sheet to the easel using Blu-Tack. Cut the card into rectangles, each measuring 9cm x 3cm.

What to do
Sit the children in a semicircle around the easel and talk about magical fairy stories. Tell them that the stories can contain all sorts of magical things because they are not real. Tell the children that they are going to make up their own magic story. Help them to read the words on the photocopiable sheet using shared reading. Ask the children to suggest ideas for filling in the spaces, reminding them that the ideas can be as weird and as wonderful as they like! Accept several suggestions for each space, and write each one on a separate piece of card. Stick these in place using Blu-Tack and read through the different versions of the story with the children.

Individual recording
Discuss with each child which words they would like to write in the spaces on their copy of the photocopiable sheet. Write the word faintly in each space for the child to write over.

Ask each child to think of a title for their story, then write this on a separate piece of paper for the child to trace over to make a cover. Encourage the child to draw a picture on the cover and to add glitter to decorate it. Help each child fix their 'cover' on top of the sheet using a stapler to create a book.

Support
Write the words in the spaces for the children.

Extension
Let older children fill in the spaces by copying the words from another piece of paper or by using their own level of emergent spelling. Ask each child to read their story aloud while other children mime the actions.

Assessment
Can the child suggest appropriate words to write in the spaces to complete the story? Can she use her imagination to suggest several ideas for each space?

Home links
Let each child make a magic wand by covering a garden cane or a piece of dowelling with aluminium foil. Cover a star template with silver foil and attach it to the wand using sticky tape. Let the children take home their wands to do some 'magic'.

Encourage the children to tell everyone about their magic the next day.

It's magic!

One night, a little ☐ went to bed. A magic ☐ flew through the window. The little ☐ climbed onto the back of the magic ☐. They flew through the dark ☐. They flew all the way to ☐. The little ☐ and the magic ☐ ☐ and ☐ all night long. In the end they flew back to the little ☐ house. The little ☐ went to bed and the magic ☐ flew away.

Bedtime story

Learning objective
To make up a bedtime story for a teddy bear.

Group size
Up to three children.

What you need
A teddy bear; doll-sized covers or blankets; doll's bed; pencils; crayons; collage materials; a copy of the photocopiable sheet for each child.

Preparation
Prepare the doll's bed with the covers or blankets and place the teddy in the bed.

What to do
Tell the children that they are going to pretend to be Mummy Bear or Daddy Bear, and they are going to make up a story in their head to tell to Baby Bear at bedtime. Tell them that you will pretend to be Mummy or Daddy Bear first and will practise with each child as they pretend to be Baby Bear.

Choose a child to be Baby Bear. Help the child to think through the story by asking key questions about the story's opening, main character, where the character lives, the main event, how the character feels and the ending of the story. If necessary, offer two or three possible answers for the child to choose from, until he gains confidence. For example, say 'Baby Bear, how would you like this story to begin? How about 'Once upon a time...', 'One night...' or 'One morning...'? Who would you like this story to be about? How about a baby animal or a little boy or little girl?'

When you have prompted the first child in this way, give the bear to the child to put to bed, then encourage the child to be Mummy Bear or Daddy Bear and to tell a bedtime story to Baby Bear.

Individual recording
Ask each child to remember the opening of their story. Faintly, write the opening in the speech bubble on the photocopiable sheet, followed by dots. Ask the child to write over the words and then to dictate the rest of the story as you write it for them on the back of their sheet. Ask the child to decorate Baby Bear's quilt cover and curtains with crayons and collage materials.

Support
Write the child's opening to their story in the speech bubble and the rest of their story on the back of the sheet. Encourage them to read the words in the speech bubble with you.

Extension
Write the child's chosen story opening on a piece of paper for the child to copy in the speech bubble. Help the child to write the rest of the story on the back of the sheet using their own level of emergent writing.

Assessment
Ask the child to choose a doll to represent himself. Let him pretend to be an adult who must put the 'child' to bed and make up a bedtime story. How much of the story can he make up independently? How much prompting does he need? Does the child use story language, such as 'and then', 'and in the end'?

Home links
Ask parents to swap places with their child and pretend to be the one being put to bed and having a bedtime story read to them. Ask them to encourage their child to tell them a story by prompting with questions.

Bedtime story

Name _____

Skills development chart

I can make up a story with picture cards

I can make up a story linking three different events

I can make up a story using props

I can make up a story about a busy day

I can make up a story with different beginnings

I can make up a story about a song or rhyme

I can make up different endings to fairy-tales

I can make up a story using three link phrases

I can make up a story about feelings

I can make up names for animal characters

I can feel like somebody in a story

I can make up a magical story

I can talk about where story people live

I can make up a bedtime story for a teddy bear

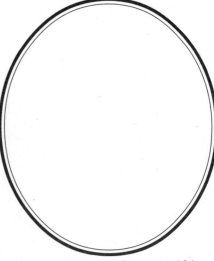

Draw a picture of yourself here.